BENEDETTO CROCE
An Autobiography

BENEDETTO CROCE
An Autobiography

Translated from the Italian by

R. G. COLLINGWOOD

With a Preface by

J. A. SMITH

BOOKS FOR LIBRARIES PRESS
FREEPORT, NEW YORK

First Published 1927
Reprinted 1970

STANDARD BOOK NUMBER:

8369-5276-6

LIBRARY OF CONGRESS CATALOG CARD NUMBER:

79-114871

PRINTED IN THE UNITED STATES OF AMERICA

PREFATORY NOTE

IT is now nearly twenty years ago that the attention of those who in this country are interested in the progress of philosophic thought in other countries of Europe began to be drawn towards Italy. For a time that attention was dispersed over the whole field or caught by what proved to be figures of minor importance; but it was not long before it was arrested and focussed upon those of Croce and Gentile. The watchers of the philosophic heavens became aware that in the Italian quarter there had appeared a new and increasing source of light which, like that of two planets in close conjunction, gradually resolved itself into its two components, each of which on nearer examination disclosed to the view of observers a new world of thoughts. Or perhaps it would be historically more correct to say that what was seen at first was the aspect of it which belongs to the mind of Croce, and it was a little later that that which

belongs to that of Gentile emerged from behind
it and revealed itself as another luminary
whose features resembled but were also different
from those of its companion. At any rate it
became evident that a new and important
development of philosophic thought had begun
and was proceeding in contemporary Italy.
During the twenty years since the evidences
of this movement were first descried, despite
the distractions due to the War, the study of
the works of these its leaders, and imprimis
of Croce, has engaged an increasing number
of competently equipped scholars, and interest
in or curiosity about them has continued
to spread among the British reading public.
There has been a call from those who do not
read Italian for introductions to a knowledge
of their doctrines, and in some measure that
demand is in course of being met. Thus their
general lineaments are becoming familiar,
although their doctrines are still far from
being clearly and distinctly apprehended, or
appreciated in their full importance.

To many or most English students of

*philosophy the discovery that there had arisen
in Italy philosophic thinkers of a magnitude
comparable with those of Germany, France,
or England itself, came as a surprise. We
had allowed ourselves to become accustomed
to regard the Italian genius as having its
gifts and talents in other spheres than that
of philosophic speculation—an unreflecting
judgement formed and held in mere forgetful-
ness and ignorance. The sympathy here with
the long struggle of Italy in the mid and
late nineteenth century for political freedom
and unity had been lively and widespread.
There had been during that struggle much
intercourse and intercommunication between
men of light and leading in the two countries. This was accompanied or followed by
a reawakening of interest in Italian history, literature, and art. Later the increased
facilities of travel made the soil of Italy
familiar ground to many Englishmen. The
extant monuments and memorials that bore
witness to the magnificent achievements of
her people in antiquity and in the Middle*

Ages received their due meed of admiration and delighted appreciation. But as the facts and features of her modern age were approached there was, it must be confessed, a sharp decline in interest and sympathy, and consequently in understanding. The period in her history during and subsequent to the Renaissance was generally viewed as one of decay or even corruption, and, warmly as her efforts to renew her youth were welcomed, the actual results were regarded as not a little disappointing. Upon modern Italy we tended to look with friendly but disenchanted eyes. In spite of the efforts of a small band of devoted and un-discouraged lovers of Italy, there was among Englishmen no lively curiosity even about its doings and farings, and very little expecta-tion of contributions from it to the general stock of European learning, enlightenment, or wisdom. Our acquaintance with what was taking place in the higher regions of modern Italian life and thought was extremely slight and superficial. Thus the beginnings of the important speculations which culminate in

*the philosophic systems of Croce and Gentile
escaped our notice, and when they came before
us in the form of large and highly articulated
structures they found us almost wholly unprepared for their reception. This ignorance and
unpreparedness was not confined to English
observers of the signs of the times. The same
was the case in Germany and France.*

*The consequence was that to all such ob-
servers it proved an embarrassingly difficult
task to determine the place and to estimate
the worth of these unexpected luminaries. In
this difficulty they were not wholly without
excuse or guilty of mere carelessness and in-
difference. Till their appearance, for some
time that quarter of the sky had been empty
of stars of the first or even the second order
of magnitude, and presented little more than
faint nebulae. Occasional explorers of the
field of recent philosophic literature found
not much more to report than what appeared
to be belated attempts to refurbish outworn
scholasticisms or pale and ambiguous reflections of foreign positivisms. As a general*

impression this was not incorrect, though it involved a certain unfairness to some individual Italian thinkers. It must also be borne in mind that the low estate of philosophical studies was at that time almost universal in Europe. But there was much less excuse for the judgement, too hastily based upon this temporary phenomenon, that there was in the Italian mind a native incapacity for such studies. To speak of such national or racial disabilities is in itself foolish enough, but here to assume or infer it could only be done by those who in the first place had forgotten, or never known of, the works of Aquinas, of Campanella and Bruno and Vico, and in the second place had restricted the evidence upon which they founded their judgement to the writings of academic or professed 'philosophers', ignoring the manner in which the same spirit lived and operated in the works of men of science like Galileo, or artistic and literary critics like Francesco de Sanctis. We are all and at all times only too apt to under-estimate the manner in

which that spirit works and progresses out
of sight and elsewhere than in such treatises
as endeavour from time to time to sum up
and systematize its manifold but widely
severed contributions to its total or integral
advance.

For all these reasons it was almost un-
avoidable that those who found themselves
presented with the systematic expression by
Croce of the results of his long meditations
on Aesthetic, Logic, Economics, Ethics, and
Philosophy in general, should make large mistakes about it, should misconceive the background from which it emerged, misanalyse
the influences which went to shape it, mis-
place it in the philosophical landscape, and
misjudge its affiliation to its predecessors.
By some or most it was hastily classed and
labelled as a form of Hegelianism or neo-
Hegelianism, and its ancestry traced to a
German source. This characterization and
pedigree seemed to be supported by the knowledge that its author was of Naples, where,
as was known, the University on its re-

foundation in 1861 had been dominated by Hegelian ideas and ideals; and it was further confirmed when it was learned that Croce was a kinsman of Bertrando Spaventa, the almost avowed Hegelian who was the first professor of philosophy there. It was too lightly assumed that he himself must be a professor of philosophy, carrying on, or being carried on by, a local academic tradition, and representing a school or group. All these were natural mistakes. It was perhaps difficult for professional or professorial philosophers to persuade themselves that a layman could be capable of taking so large a view, could have acquired or possessed so ample an acquaintance with past speculations, or could have either cared or been able to give to his thoughts a form so methodical and systematic as they found in the successive volumes of Croce's Filosofia dello Spirito. *Nor was it anything but natural that they should suppose that what was there offered to them had the same sort of origin and the same sort of foundation as what they themselves were* engaged in constructing for the use of themselves and their pupils. These erroneous impressions might have been corrected had they extended their reading of his works beyond these volumes. But some of this evidence was not easily accessible to them, and the published records of Croce's multifarious critical and historical work seemed irrelevant to their special concern with his philosophy. De me quoque fabula narratur, and I now recognize that the result of such careless ignorance or wilful ignoring was to create an error in perspective which falsified many of the features of Croce's system and led to misconstructions in regard to its relations of time and place and affiliation to other systems, and so in important ways distorted our view of it. The order in which the several parts of it came before us generated and fostered some of these misunderstandings. The first part of it with which we became acquainted was his Aesthetic—his theory of the nature of Art. This was indeed the first part of it which was elaborated and presented to the world. But

it came before us—or we so took it—as complete in itself and isolated or divorced from
a context in which it lived in Croce's own
mind, and which, though it was not developed,
was sufficiently intimated in his presentment
of it. But our ears were too dull to catch
the significance of the hints and clues he
there supplied to us. Even when the other
parts were in the subsequent volumes similarly elaborated, and the whole system displayed on a wide canvas, it still presented itself
to us as a result without much trace upon it
of its origin or the process of its development,
and with only slight and elusive indications
of its roots and filaments in concrete experience. Behind and beneath lay something without knowledge of which we could not fully
comprehend it and concerning which we could
form only uncertain and unverifiable conjectures. It was indeed no idle curiosity that led
us to indulge in such conjectures, but we
certainly had little right to call upon the author
to furnish more information about such circumstances than he felt inclined to communi-

cate. *To him doubtless they had faded out of memory or retired into the background and the margin, accompanying his advance like a faint halo surrounding the lighted path which he trod.*

It was a piece of good fortune for us that in 1915 he paused to look back and around and before in order to see clearly where he had come to stand. The work now presented by his permission to English readers was written, as indeed might be said of all his works, primarily for himself. It was not published, but printed in a small number of copies and distributed by him among a few to whom he thought it would be of interest and service. It is now made available for the large and increasing circle of his English readers, and for this they owe him a debt of gratitude.

Ten years have elapsed since the date of its composition. During all these its author has continued his multifarious activities with undiminished zest and vigour. His work has not merely increased in bulk only, or only enriched itself with organic detail. He has

incessantly reviewed his previously won re-
sults, modifying and reshaping them to meet
the ever-new demands made upon his sys-
tematic thinking. His doctrines have under-
gone changes that to many appear to amount
to revolutions, and, if not the whole structure
of his system, at least large portions of it,
have been all but demolished and recon-
structed. But in fact, what has happened
is that his thought has continued to evolve
under the pressure of new problems and the
demands made upon it by novel and unan-
ticipated situations. Thus it manifests its
vitality and fertility, and that not merely
in inspiring and guiding its first discoverer's
unwearied and diverse labours; its quicken-
ing and heartening and enlightening spirit
extends ever more widely not only into the
whole intellectual and moral life of his
country but also far beyond its borders. It
is beginning to acquire a range of influence
almost as wide as Europe, in most countries
of which it has enlisted a band of students,
expositors, and critics.

To many it appears as a restoration to its throne of the spirit of the great Idealistic systems of the early nineteenth century. But if so, that spirit has returned, not like the Bourbons 'having learned nothing and forgotten nothing', but on the contrary strengthened and enriched by the whole practical and theoretic experience through which during that century it has passed. Above all it has profited by that intense and various preoccupation with history which, far more than its impressive development of the sciences, characterizes and distinguishes this from previous periods. Croce has set himself to interpret the modern mind to itself as in and through its more recent experience it has formed itself, and his philosophy is like a search-light cast upon our present minds and our present world. It professes no more than to illuminate the present and disclaims all doctrines concerning primordial origins and ultimate ends, eschewing all archaeologies and transcendentalisms and eschatologies, and concentrating itself upon the interpreta-

tion of that history which the spirit of Man incessantly enacts and creates.

In each country the students of philosophy must first and for long go to school with those teachers who share their national experiences and speak their native tongue, and we in this country have no lack of men who are of the front rank, such as Green and Caird and Bosanquet and Bradley. But it would be great unwisdom in the spirit of a narrow nationalism to neglect those who have performed or are performing the same office elsewhere, and now it is the precept of wisdom to make and increase our acquaintance with the teaching of Croce, an acquaintance to which this short but pregnant work is an open door.

J. A. Smith.

Oxford, *Jan.* 1926.

I. WHAT IS, AND WHAT IS NOT, CONTAINED IN THIS BOOK

HAVING now reached my fiftieth year, I have determined to employ the ideal pause in my spiritual life which that date brings with it in looking back at the road I have traversed, and trying to fix my eyes on that which I have still to traverse in the years of work that lie before me.

But what I shall here set down will be neither confessions, nor recollections, nor memoirs. Not confessions, or a moral self-examination ; for though I think it valuable to confess oneself hourly, that is, to arrive at a clear consciousness of one's own acts at the moment of doing them, I see no value in passing a general moral judgement upon one's life as a whole. Apart from the single aim of discovering whether one does or does not deserve heaven or purgatory, I do not see what purpose these general confessions can serve, except perhaps that of flattering one's vanity; either the vanity of complacent self-approbation or the vanity of self-accusation and lamentation over one's misdeeds; vanity in either case, because based in either case on an exaggerated opinion of one's own importance. And further, when one tries conscientiously to answer the question whether one has been good or bad, one soon finds oneself on slippery ground; for in framing a judgement of this kind one perpetually oscillates between the temptations to flatter oneself and to libel oneself. The reason for this dilemma lies in the fact already stated : that the individual man by himself, apart from the whole, is a very little thing; and hence it follows that not only others but even he himself cannot but overlook the greater part of the things he has done and the feelings that moved him to do them; and in the attempt to collect them and compose them into a picture he may easily so colour them in the light of his present favourable or unfavourable feelings as to form an imaginary presentation of them which, later, fades and dissolves beneath the questionings of self-criticism, leaving him at last in doubt as to what he should rightly think.

Nor shall I set down my recollections; for though the past fills me with emotion and with melancholy, I should not think myself justified in putting these feelings on paper unless I regarded myself as a poet; unless, that is to say, these feelings formed the centre of gravity of my being and the objects of my best spiritual faculties. No doubt, I am often led to dream of my past; but these dreams are brief and fleeting, soon dispelled by the demands of my work, which is not a poet's work. If I so far gave way to my dreams as to put these recollections, for which a silent discourse with myself is sufficient, into the form of writing, or discourse addressed to others, I should only be falling back into the other alternative, the trivial vanity of confessions, and incurring the well-deserved contempt which is the usual reward of attempts to interest other people in the things that have happened to oneself, in one's own transient personality.

Lastly, I shall not write my memoirs. Memoirs are the chronicle of one's life and the lives of the men with whom one has worked or whom one has seen and known, and events in which one has taken part; and people write them in the hope of preserving for posterity important facts which otherwise would be forgotten. But the chronicle of my life, so far as it contains anything worth recording, is contained in the chronology and bibliography of my written works; and since I have taken no part, either as actor or as witness, in events of another kind, I have little or nothing to say of the men I have known or the things I have seen.

What, then, am I to write, if not confessions or recollections or memoirs? I
will try in plain terms to sketch a criticism, and therefore a history, of myself;
that is, of the contribution which, like
every other man, I have made to the
common stock of work done : the history
of my 'calling' or 'mission'. If these
words seem pretentious, I have already
qualified them by pointing out that every
man contributes something to the common stock of work; every man has his
calling or mission, and may write its history; though it is true that if I had done
nothing but attend to my private con-
cerns and those of my family, or—still
more—if I had fulfilled only the humble
mission of one who had enjoyed what
he could get, I should not now be taking
up my pen to give an account of myself.

Why, in a word, after composing so
many critical and historical essays on
writers of the present day and of the
past, trying to understand the character

of each and his development, and to discover what in him was original and personal to him, should I not write an essay on myself? The answer is easy: Leave others to speak of you. And so I do, whenever they like; but in order that they may speak with better knowledge and more truth, and even with a more enlightened severity of judgement, I will tell them what I know of my work, persuaded that by so doing I shall call their attention to facts which else they might have missed or only discovered with difficulty, just as I for my part no doubt miss others which they can easily detect.

Above all, I cannot pass judgement upon myself from a point of view which rises superior to my own limitations; for clearly, though I can criticize my past in the light of my present, I cannot judge my present in the light of the future. And therefore it cannot be helped if some of these pages present the appearance of a defence or justification of the work which, whatever its character, I have done. It cannot be helped, because even if now I were to condemn this work in the name of a new consciousness that has since arisen in me, I should yet be condemning it from the point of view of the present, and this would imply in some sense a justification or consecration of the past, of those acts and experiences which have led me to a better present. This is an inherent and logical implication of the task I have taken in hand; it must not be set down to the effects of pride.

II. OUTWARD EVENTS AND
INNER LIFE

WHEN I look back at my earliest childhood and try to discern there the first premonitions of my later growth, I recollect the eagerness with which I asked for, and listened to, every kind of story; the pleasure that I took in the first books of fiction and history that were given to me or fell into my hands; and the love that I felt for books in themselves, in their material presence. At the age of six or seven years I knew no greater delight than that of going with my mother into a book-shop, gazing enraptured at the volumes arranged on the shelves, following with anxious eyes those which the bookseller laid out on the counter for my choice, and carrying home my new treasures, revelling in their delicious smell of printed paper. My mother had never lost her love for the books, mostly romances of medieval life, which she had read as a girl in her home in the Abruzzi; and by the time I was nine years old I had studied this branch of literature from the tales of good Canon Schmidt to the novels of Madame Cotti and Tommaso Grossi, my favourites at that time. I remember once expressing the opinion to my school-fellows, during a discussion on military exploits, that there had been only two great warriors, Malek-Adel and Marco Visconti. My mother was also a lover of art and of the monuments of anti-quity; and it was the visits which, with her, I made to the churches of Naples, pausing to examine pictures and tombs, that first aroused in me an interest in the past. Throughout my childhood I had, as it were, a heart within my heart; and this heart, my most intimate and cher-ished passion, was literature; or rather, history.

But though my whole family set me

an example of peace, order, and industry,
my father always shut in his study among
his business papers, my mother always
first up in the morning and going about
the house helping the maids and direct-
ing their work, it brought to my ears
no echo of public life or politics. My
grandfather had been a staunch old-
fashioned magistrate, devoted to the
Bourbons; my father acted on the tradi-
tional principle of honest Neapolitans,
that a gentleman ought to mind his own
business and that of his family, and keep
out of political squabbles. I used to hear
them praise Ferdinand II as a good king
grossly slandered, and Maria Cristina as a
saint, and I seldom heard the authors of
the Risorgimento named, and never without reservations, expressions of distrust,
or even satirical remarks about liberal
windbags and self-seeking 'patriots'.

A Jesuit who was for a short time
my mother's confessor suggested that she
should read Father Bresciani's novels, and

give them to me to read; and they inspired me with a sentimental admiration
for the picturesque papal zouaves and a
corresponding dislike of the drab Pied-
montese. The two Spaventas were indeed
cousins of my father; but we had practic-
ally ceased to be on speaking terms with
one of them, Bertrando, who was an ex-
priest, and whom my father's mother and
sister had heard—as they used to relate
in a rather scandalized manner—celebrat-
ing mass in our house; and when, a few
years later, I began to attend the University, my mother took me aside and warned
me not to go to Spaventa's lectures, fearing
lest they should pervert my mind from
the principles of religion. I disobeyed
her, and attended some harmless lectures
of his on formal logic, but without ven-
turing to introduce myself to him; and
he died about the same time, and never
knew that somewhere among the crowded
audience was a cousin of his own.

With Silvio, too, we were on unfriendly

terms. He had offended my father by a supercilious manner or a cutting remark; for he looked down upon his cousin as a man with no interest in politics or in anything but his land.

The political atmosphere, so to speak, which was lacking in my home, was equally absent from my school. This was a Catholic school, which I entered at the age of a little over nine years. It was not a Jesuit school; it supplied a sound moral and religious education, free from superstition and fanaticism; but it was a school kept by priests and much patronized by the aristocrats of the Bourbon party, and the nearest approach it made towards the ideal of a united Italy was a lingering interest in the doctrines of Neo-Guelfism, which some of the priests on the staff had embraced in their younger days. In 1876, my first year, the centenary of Legnano was celebrated by a speech-day; and at these speech-days and at the regular prize-givings we almost always saw the *abate*

Tosti, a great survivor of the Neo-Guelf movement, who pinned more than one medal upon my school jacket. Of the revolutions, the conspiracies, the '48, the '59, and the '60, Cavour, Mazzini, and Garibaldi, I knew in a sense during my schooldays; but they were mere names to me; their historical reality and their ideal significance were discoveries which I made for myself later, at the close of my youth.

To these circumstances of my childhood I attribute, at least in part, the relatively late development in me of political feelings and political ideals, suppressed as they were for many years by absorption in literature and scholarship. But every defect has its compensations, and I suppose that I owe to the same causes my critical attitude towards all legends inspired by political interests, my contempt for the cant of Liberalism, and my hatred of pompous phrases and all rhetorical ostentation, together with my respect for sound and useful measures, from whatever party they may proceed.

In addition to this taste for letters and history, I experienced during my school-days fleeting impulses of asceticism, or rather, transitory promptings towards a life of piety, and some pain at my inability fully to obey the commands of religion, especially the injunction to love God and not only to fear him. Fear him I did, in terrifying visions of the torments of hell; but I found the idea of a lovable God too abstract to grasp. Of the weekly confession which I was bound by the rules of the college to make every Saturday, I can recall nothing except a laborious effort at accuracy, which ultimately led me to make notes of my 'sins' for the week on a piece of paper; and, on one occasion only, a sincere act of contrition on hearing, I know not whether truly or no, of the wretched state into which a poor priest had fallen, who was once our 'prefect of studies' and had been dismissed by the director for a rebellion into which he had been led with childish treachery by myself and my companions.

In the class-room I was always among the best performers. Before entering the school I had already read so much that I never made the mistakes of spelling for which my schoolfellows' exercise-books underwent constant correction, and it cost me no effort to grasp and remember what I was taught; my successes therefore were easily won. And since I was a spirited boy and often in trouble for breaches of discipline, my masters in their admonitions used to contrast my conduct in 'class' with my conduct in 'dormitory'. But in the rough-and-tumble of school life I found that those who had claws with which to defend themselves were always able to win respect; and when I think of that lesson, and of the boyish feelings of loyalty and honour which are fostered by living in contact with contemporaries of widely different characters,

I can never join in the fashionable out-
cry against boarding-school education or
agree in thinking it better for boys to be
brought up at home.

I took my *liceo* course as a day-boy,
while still at the school; and now began
a religious crisis, which I carefully concealed from my family, and even from
my friends, regarding it as a shameful
weakness. It was brought about neither
by irreligious literature, nor by malicious
insinuations, as pious persons commonly
believe and declare, nor even by the
words of philosophers like Spaventa, but
by no less a person than the principal of
the school, a sincere priest and a learned
theologian, who most unwisely delivered
a course of lectures upon what he called
the 'philosophy of religion' to us *liceo*
students, to confirm us in the faith. They
worked upon my mind, hitherto un-
touched by such problems, like a ferment.
This weakening of my faith caused me
much grief and lively apprehensions. As

a sick man searches for medicine, I sought out books on apologetics, but they left me cold. At times I found comfort in the words of truly religious minds; for example, in reading Pellico's *Le mie prigioni*, whose pages I sometimes, in an ecstasy of joy, kissed for very gratitude; and then—my thoughts wandered elsewhere, life claimed my attention, I no longer asked myself whether I believed or no, even while through force of habit or for the sake of convenience I kept up certain religious observances; till at last, little by little, I let even these drop, and a day came when I saw, and told myself plainly, that I was done with my religious beliefs.

In the second and third classes of the *liceo*, too, my literary ambitions received their first gratification. Book-lover as I was, and already a collector of old and rare books, I passed for a scholar; and reading literary journals, and especially Martini's *Fanfulla della domenica*, which

was then a quite new and very valuable
thing in Italy, I took to modelling my
compositions upon the straightforward
style of these journals, as more suited to
my turn of mind than the poetic or em-
phatic style, which from that time forward I have never again even tried to
adopt. I noticed in myself a certain dry-
ness and baldness of expression, and envied
some of my companions for the richness
of their style ; but now that I look back
upon it I see that this baldness was not
a bad sign, accompanied as it was by a
kind of logical power and striving after
sincerity which prevented me from doing
violence to myself. At times I composed
'sketches' in the style of the day, and
satirical invectives ; but for the most part
I wrote critical essays, a few of which I
published in a literary journal in 1882
and have since reissued in a slender volume called *Il primo passo*,[1] of which a few

[1] *Il primo passo: IV scritti critici*, Naples, 1910:
50 numbered copies printed.

copies were printed. During this period
I read and re-read the works of De Sanctis
and Carducci; but though I learnt from
De Sanctis a few guiding principles of
literary criticism, I cared little in those
days for his firm and balanced moral
character, and was much more attracted
by the violent and combative attitudes
of Carducci. I even tried to imitate
him in a contempt for the frivolous and
self-indulgent manners of the fashionable
world—a contempt which found a ready
target in those of my schoolfellows who
belonged to Neapolitan society—and in
a kind of ideal of class-warfare; but this
was always in me a superficial pose, un-
supported by serious moral convictions.

My domestic life suffered a violent
catastrophe and a profound breach of
continuity by the earthquake of Casamic-
ciola in 1883, in which I lost both my
parents and my only sister, and lay buried
for some hours beneath the ruins, injured
in several places. When I had to some

extent recovered, I went with my brother to Rome to live with Silvio Spaventa, who had taken upon himself the office of guardian. It was an act whose true value I only came to understand afterwards. Spaventa, immersed though he was in political affairs, and not living, of late years, on the best of terms with my father, felt it his duty to act as protector towards the two boys who alone survived out of a family in which he himself, when a boy, had been surrounded with affectionate kindness.

My first years at Rome were like a bad dream. I found myself in a society utterly different from that to which I had been accustomed, in the house of a politician of high standing, among deputies and professors and journalists, his guests, and surrounded by discussions on politics, law, and science, and the lively echoes of parliamentary debates and conflicts. The house was in the Via della Missione, next to the Palazzo di Montecitorio. I was quite unprepared to find a place within myself for this new form of life; and the public policy of the time—it was 1884 and 1885, the years of the Depretis ministry—and the sarcastic way in which it was attacked and reviled by Spaventa and his friends and visitors, did little to restore my confidence, to arouse my enthusiasm, or to lift me from the depression into which I had fallen. Stunned by the domestic tragedy that had overtaken me, ailing in body and, though suffering from no one definite disease, appearing to suffer from all at once, perplexed as to myself and the path I ought to take, racked by doubts concerning the purpose and meaning of life and similar problems of youth, I lost all lightness of heart and faith in the future, and was tempted to think myself faded before I had flowered, old before I had been young. These were the darkest and most bitter years of my life; the only ones in which at evening, laying my head upon my pillow,

I often ardently wished that I might
not awake in the morning, and even
formed thoughts of suicide. I had no
friends and no amusements; I never once
saw Rome at night. I entered my name
at the university for the course in law,
but never studied with any diligence and
never sat for the examination. It gave
me more pleasure to shut myself up in
the libraries, especially the Casanatense,
which was still kept by Dominican monks
and had upon its desks ink-pots with great
stoppers, dredgers filled with golden sand,
and quill pens; and there I used to pursue
researches into subjects chosen by myself,
inventing my methods and preliminaries
as I went along, hesitating, making mistakes, working too little at some things
and too much at others. I made frequent
attempts to improve my mind, but only
took a subject up to lay it down again
and take up another, chaotically, not
because the vigour of my mind drove me
this way and that, but because I did not

know how to work, and had neither the docility of the pupil nor the confident and passionate energy of the self-taught scholar.

In the second year of my stay at Rome, I resolved to attend Antonio Labriola's lectures on moral philosophy. I already knew Labriola as a frequent evening visitor at Spaventa's house, where I had listened with great admiration to his conversation, sparkling with energy and wit and overflowing with original ideas. His lectures, all unexpectedly, came as the answer to my urgent longing for a new and rational faith concerning life and its purposes and duties. I had lost the guidance of religious doctrines, and at the same time I felt myself in danger of infection from materialistic, sensationalistic, and associationist theories ; though as to the true nature of these I was under no illusion, and saw clearly enough that at bottom they were a mere negation of morality and resolved it into a more

or less veiled egoism. Labriola's Herbartian ethics achieved for me the restoration of the majesty of the ideal, the *ought
to be* as opposed to the *is*, mysterious
in this opposition, but by the very
opposition absolute and uncompromising.
I used to summarize Labriola's lectures in
a few headings, written down on paper
and reflected upon when I awoke next
morning ; and this was the time at which
I most earnestly laboured at the ideas of
pleasure and duty, purity and impurity,
actions rendered attractive by the pure
moral ideal and actions endowed with
an apparent moral value by psychological
association, habit, or the impulse of passion. These antitheses I examined in the
light of a kind of experiments made upon
myself, in the light of self-observation
and self-condemnation; and many years
afterwards all these thoughts found their
way, in a clarified theoretical form, into
my *Philosophy of Practice*, a book which,
because of its connexion with these

memories, has to my eyes almost the appearance of an autobiography, though this is wholly concealed from the reader by the systematic form of its exposition.

Yet if I had to describe the plan of life which existed in my mind at the time of which I am speaking, I should have to call it pessimistic. On the one hand, my plan consisted of work in the field of literature and scholarship, undertaken partly from natural inclination and partly from a desire to do something in the world ; on the other, in the fulfilment of moral duties, especially understood as works of compassion. It contained elements drawn from the spirit of Christianity, especially a sort of fear of enjoyment and happiness as faults deserving punishment or demanding pardon ; and it also, as I realised later, contained elements of egotism, since the true compassion, the highest benevolence, is that which tries to bring its whole self into

harmony with the ends of reality and
compel others to move towards the same
ends; and goodness of heart is only goodness in a true and worthy sense when
accompanied by an ever-widening and
ever-deepening insight into things. But
this contemptible ideal was the best of
which I was capable in my depressed state
of mind. Though working at philosophy
and reading some philosophical books
to aid my thoughts, it never occurred to
me that this spontaneous mental impulse
might be pointing out the road on which
I should put forth my best efforts and enjoy my purest pleasures and highest con-
solations—should find, in a word, my
calling. I was driven to philosophy by
the longing to assuage my misery and to
give an orientation to my moral and intellectual life. Scholar, collector of anecdota, man of letters, involuntary dabbler
in philosophy—all these features confusedly make up the picture of myself
presented in some slight essays of this

period, which I have collected into another volume called *Iuvenilia*.[1]

Not only did I fail to recognize my philosophical calling, but the glimpse of it which I had sometimes half enjoyed faded almost completely when I went back to Naples in 1886. My life became more regular, and my mind calmer and at times almost happy ; but this was because I had left behind me the bitterness and passion of Roman political circles and entered a society of librarians, keepers of archives, scholars, antiquaries, and suchlike good, worthy, gentle souls, old or middle-aged men for the most part, not much given to thinking; and to this society I adapted myself and, outwardly at any rate, adopted its ways. For the next few years I might be said to be carrying out, to some extent, the plan I had formed at Rome. My life was wholly given up to antiquarian studies. I travelled

[1] *Iuvenilia*, 1883–1887. Bari, Laterza, 1914: 100 numbered copies.

to Germany, Spain, France, and England,
but always as a scholar and man of letters;
and my social duties, as I then understood
them, I performed with very little enthusiasm. For some time I undertook the
administration of my family estate, but I
never worked at it lovingly and intelli-
gently, as my father had done, and I tried
to arrange the work in such a way as to
spare myself most of the trouble. The
political life of my country was a mere
spectacle which I watched with no intention of taking active part in it; I hardly
even joined in it to the extent of having
feelings and opinions about it. I took a
certain interest in what was called the
'social problem'; but even that I only
regarded as a problem of abstract ethics.
The philosophical questionings of my
youth had been driven into a dark recess
of my spirit, from which words of re-
proach would issue from time to time,
calling me to a more serious life; and
chivalry compelled me to speak up in

defence of philosophical studies whenever
I heard my new Neapolitan friends de-
riding them, which they often did. In
certain moods turning inwardly upon myself I tried to read books of philosophy;
almost always German ones, for I had acquired the cult of the German book first
from Spaventa and then from Labriola,
but I did not understand them very well,
and lost heart; for I supposed that my
failure must be due to my own fault, and
not to the inherent incomprehensibility,
the artificial character, of the systems I
was studying. Besides, I had a profound
respect for professors of philosophy; for
I further supposed that they, as specialists,
must be in actual possession of this abstruse science from whose table I had with
such pains collected a few crumbs, and I
did not know that I should find within a
few years, to my astonishment and annoyance, that most of them possessed nothing
of it whatever, not even the little that I,
by mere will to understand, had succeeded

in making my own. It was with a joyous excitement of spirits and intellect that I met Labriola again, whether in Rome or on his visits to Naples; I drank his words greedily, amplified them and commented upon them on my own account, and turned them to my own uses. But in general, apart from this secret effervescence from which a bubble came now and then to the surface, I was for six years, from 1886 to 1892, wholly turned towards the outer world, I mean towards antiquarian studies; and during that period, among other things, I composed many of the essays afterwards collected in my volume on the Neapolitan Revolution of 1799; my annals of the Neapolitan theatre from the Renaissance to the end of the eighteenth century; fragments of a book on the eighteenth century in Naples, which now figure as 'eighteenth-century portraits and anecdota' in my volume of papers on seventeenth-century literature, and other essays making up a series of 'historical

curiosities '. I also set on foot, at my own
expense, the publication of a 'library of
Neapolitan literature', and started, with
a few friends, a review called *Napoli
nobilissima*, dealing with topographical
questions and the history of art, in which
some of my ' Neapolitan histories and
legends' first appeared.

Apart from any service they may have
rendered to the increase of knowledge in
the narrow field with which they dealt,
and considered only in their relation to
myself and my spiritual life, I can now see
in these works a certain positive value :
first, the delight with which I called up
these pictures of the past in a flight of
youthful imagination, insatiable in its
quest of dreams and of exercise for its
literary powers; secondly, the persistent
and conscientious research by which, as
a formal discipline, I schooled myself to
labour in the service of knowledge. The
same characteristic reappears in the zeal
with which I took part in *L'Archivio storico*

and in *Napoli nobilissima*, and planned
collections and editions of authors.

But the negative aspect of these works
was of far greater importance for my
spiritual development. The energy with
which, during these years, I threw myself
into the collection of anecdota and antiquarian details, the satiety that followed
their collection, and the disgust that followed the satiety, all helped to strengthen
the feeling, driven into a corner of my
mind but never extinguished, that knowledge ought to have a form and a value
very different from that possessed by
these external essays in literary scholarship, and that unless that which we do is
profitable, our glory is in vain. At the
very moment of publishing the more important of the works just enumerated, and
so making my entry upon the stage of
literature, surrounded by congratulation,
praise, and encouragement, and hailed as
one of the 'hopes' of sound Italian
studies, at that very moment my sense of

revolt and of inner alienation from these 'sound studies' reached its climax; reached such a degree of intensity as amounted to injustice towards them and towards myself.

With the publication of these works I seem to have closed a period of my life; to have arrived at a point at which I must now do something more serious and, as I put it at the time, more 'inward'. I was still ignorant of the real, ultimate reason for my discontent, and therefore hoped to find this seriousness and inwardness in a new work which should break through the narrow and trivial limits of municipal history and rise to the height of national history. This I planned to treat not as political history, but—to quote once more my words of the time—as moral history, understood not as a chronicle of events but as the history of the feelings and spiritual life of Italy from the Renaissance onwards. Thinking that such a history could not be written without

special knowledge of the relations between Italy and other countries and an
inquiry into their mutual 'influences', I
set myself to investigate, as at once a part
and a preliminary of my more general
task, the influence of Spain on Italian life,
by means of detailed studies in Italian
and Spanish literature and with the help
of the skill which by now I possessed in
unearthing materials from manuscripts
and little-known books. At the same time
I recognized the gaps in my historical and
literary education, and made up my mind
to fill them; but the recognition was
merely material and mechanical, and the
means I took to make good the defect
were of the same kind; and hence I soon
wearied of filling my mind with lifeless
and disconnected facts at the expense of
much toil and with no constructive result.

Once more nature proved the best
physician. In trying to find my way out
of the difficulties which beset me as to
the best method of pursuing both my

chosen task and historical studies at large, I found myself unconsciously brought by degrees face to face with the problem of the nature of history and of knowledge; and I read a number of books, Italian and German, on the philosophy and method of history, among others—for the first time—Vico's *Scienza nuova*. Since reading De Sanctis at my desk as a *liceo* student, and grappling with German aesthetics while attending Labriola's lectures on ethics at the university, I had never altogether ceased to think about questions of aesthetics; and therefore found it easy now to connect the problem of history with the problem of art.

Thus, after much hesitation and a whole series of provisional solutions, during February or March 1893, after a whole day of intense thought, I sketched in the evening an essay which I called *History subsumed under the general concept of Art.*[1] This

[1] *La Storia ridotta sotto il concetto generale dell' Arte.* Reprinted in *Primi Saggi*, Laterza, 1919.

was a kind of revelation to me of my true self. Not only did it give me the joy of seeing in a clear light certain conceptions which are commonly confused, and tracing the logical origin of numerous false tendencies, but it astonished me by the ease and heat with which I wrote it, as something close to my heart and coming straight from my heart, and not a more or less trivial and unimportant antiquarian essay. Nor was I less encouraged by the importance attached by critics to my work—which smacked of paradox and was certainly bold enough in those days of positivism—and the discussions to which it gave rise, in which I felt more than once that I had my opponents at my mercy. Yet even now I did not regard philosophical speculation as a path opening before me; and for the time being, my logical and methodological ideas set more or less in order, I plunged once more into working for my projected history, and devoted almost the whole of

1893 and 1894 to researches into the relations between Spain and Italy and my
share in *Napoli nobilissima* and similar
reviews, writing a considerable number
of preparatory studies and notes and
sketches of the book which I had in mind.
And it was only another of these unfore-
seen and irresistible impulses, or involuntary blazings-up of the mind, that led
me, while trying to expand and clarify
a discussion with a professor of philology
of my acquaintance during a visit to the
country, to write in a fortnight at the end
of 1894 a short polemical book on the
method of literary criticism,[1] which caused
a stir in my little world and plunged me
into several controversies, some lasting
for months.

I still recall the astonishment of the
old Neapolitan scholar Don Bartolommeo
Capasso, when he heard of the uproar
caused by a peaceful reader in the State

[1] *La Critica Letteraria.*   Reprinted in *Primi
Saggi*, cit.

record office, and the smile with which he called me 'a Garibaldi of criticism'. But my purpose in writing this book had been no more than to make up my mind concerning the true method of literary history, as I had already done concerning that of history in general; it was an act of personal liberation, not the first step in the career of a professional philosopher. And hence, before the controversies to which my book gave rise had died down, I was back in my studies of Italo-Spanish relations and had finished, as best I could, that part of my subject which belonged to the Middle Ages and Renaissance, and launched out on the ocean of the seventeenth century.

But no sooner had I taken up the thread of my work when, in April 1895, Labriola sent me from Rome the first of his essays on the materialistic conception of history —it was the essay on the Communists' Manifesto—to read and, if possible, publish. I read it and re-read it; and again I felt my whole mind burst into flame. New thoughts and problems took root in my spirit and so overran it that I was powerless to free myself from them. I broke off—I might almost say, gave up —my researches upon Spain in Italian life, and threw myself for several months, with inexpressible fervour, into the study of economics, of which till then I knew nothing. I paid little attention to hand-books and popular expositions, but studied the chief classics of the subject, and sought out everything in the literature of social-ism above the merely popular level ; and by resolving to master the essential points and to clear up the hardest problems I soon came to know my way about, to the surprise of Labriola, who lost no time in confessing to me his doubts concern-ing the main conceptions of socialism and explaining his attempts to restate them in a more precise theoretical form.

His surprise was shared by friends of mine, economists by profession, who were thunderstruck to find themselves more than once outmatched in conversing with me; for I had a firm hold on the fundamental conceptions and extracted their consequences with an uncompromising logic, while they knew far more than I did, but could not see the connexion between the things they knew. And the study of economics, a conception which from the point of view of Marxism is identical with that of reality as a whole, or philosophy, brought me back to philosophical problems, especially to those of ethics and logic, but also to the general conception of the spirit and its various modes of operation. These thoughts, like my economic studies, were all directed towards history as their ultimate end; for I long intended to return to my historical researches armed with my new weapons of economics and historical materialism; and I had already planned a history of southern Italy on these lines, and had begun to collect materials for it by plun-

dering cartularies and diplomatic codices.
But my acquaintance with Marxian literature and the earnest attention which I
had for some time devoted to German
and Italian socialistic periodicals had
shaken my mind and aroused in me, for
the first time in my life, a semblance of
political passion, giving me a strange new
sensation like that of a man who, when
no longer young, falls in love for the
first time and watches within him the
mysterious growth of a new passion. In
that fire I burnt my abstract moralism,
and learnt that the course of history has
the right to bend and break individuals.
My home life had not trained me to feel
enthusiasm, or even sympathy, towards
the ordinary fashionable liberalism of
Italian politics, and the criticism and
condemnation and ridicule of it to which
I had listened in Spaventa's house had
not increased my respect for it; but in
the socialistic vision of the rebirth and
redemption of mankind through labour

and in labour, I seemed to breathe a new air of faith and hope.

But this faith, this political passion, did not last. The faith was undermined by my own criticism of Marxism—a criticism the more damaging that it was meant for a defence and a restatement —expressed in a series of essays composed between 1895 and 1900 and later collected in the volume called *Historical Materialism and Marxian Economics*;[1] the passion burnt itself out because *natura tamen usque recurrit*, and mine was at bottom the nature of a student and thinker.

The excitement of those years bore good fruit in the shape of a widened experience of human problems and a quickening of philosophical activity. From that time on, philosophy played an increasing part in my studies; partly because there was henceforth a certain

---

[1] *Materialismo storico ed Economia marxistica*, Laterza; 3rd ed., 1918. E. T. *Historical Materialism, &c.*, 1914.

intellectual estrangement between myself and Labriola, who could not forgive some of the conclusions which I drew from his premises, and this gave occasion for correspondence and collaboration with Gentile, whom I had known when quite a young man, when he was a student at the university of Pisa, and who had reviewed my works on the theory of history and on Marxism and had corresponded with me about the reprinting of Bertrando Spaventa's writings. I was drawn to Gentile both by certain resemblances in our practical attitude and also by a similarity of education and mental development; for he had done his first work in the field of literary history as a pupil of D'Ancona, and was a practised philological scholar. Like myself, he took and still takes peculiar pleasure in work of this kind, which fixes the mind upon a determinate and concrete object, and is a task which cannot be entrusted to 'hacks', but must be done by his own

efforts, for his own needs, and to suit his
own purposes, by every competent student. Thus, with a broadened mind and
in far better intellectual company than
that of my early Neapolitan days, I felt
once more the impulse to throw into
shape, before doing anything else, those
long-standing meditations upon art which
in spite of distractions and interruptions
had never left me since as a schoolboy
I read De Sanctis, but had now, in the
course of my recent studies, entered into
relation with the other problems of the
spirit, and ceased to be a fit subject for
a mere isolated monograph. By setting
down what I had in my head, I thought,
I should relieve myself of a weight of
which I could not get rid by forgetting
it. I therefore made bold to plan the
writing of an Aesthetic and a history of
aesthetic, for the former of which I
imagined that I had already in my possession all, or almost all, the ideas to be set
forth. I formed this plan in the autumn

of 1898, but I had to defer carrying
it out till the following summer, being
occupied in completing various economic and historical works, and in editing
publications connected with the celebra-
tion of the centenary of the Neapolitan
revolution of 1799.[1]

But when I set to work, and began
to collect my scattered thoughts, I found
that I knew little or nothing. The gaps
in my knowledge multiplied as I looked ;
the things on which I believed myself
to have a firm hold became indistinct
and confused ; and for nearly five months
I read nothing, I walked about for hours
together, I lay for half-days and whole
days on the sofa, searching incessantly
within myself, and jotting down notes
and ideas, each a criticism of the last.
This torment became even worse when,
in November, I tried to state the fundamental propositions of aesthetic in a brief

[1] *La Rivoluzione napoletana del 1799*; Laterza,
ed. 3, 1912.

essay; for I came at least ten times, in
the course of my argument, to some point
at which I was obliged to take a step
wholly unjustified in logic, and every
time I had to go back to the beginning
to discover in my starting-point the ob-
scurity or error which had brought me
to this *impasse* : then, the error corrected,
I would go forward once more and the
same thing would happen again. Only
after six or seven months was I able to
send my essay to the press in its present
form, with the title *Fundamental Propositions of an Aesthetic, as science of expression and general theory of Language* ; [1] dry
and abstruse, but finished, and leaving
me not only with my mind made up on
the problems of the spirit, but with a
lively and confident understanding of
most of the chief problems at which the
great philosophers have worked ; an
understanding which cannot be acquired

[1] *Tesi fondamentali di un' Estetica come scienza
dell' espressione e linguistica generale*, 1900.

by reading their books but only by re-
enacting their mental drama in one's own
person, under the stimulus of actual life.

The historical part of my book was
to have followed the sketch of the theoretical; but in November 1900, when I
was about to begin working at this history, after taking a rest in reading and
working at other subjects and in a visit
to the country, a public inquiry was
made into the communal administration
of Naples, in consequence of a scandalous
trial, and an extraordinary commissioner
was appointed to carry on its work. I
was asked to assist this commissioner,
and could not well refuse; I took in hand
the administration of the elementary and
intermediate schools of the commune,
and spent all day, from eight o'clock in
the morning to eight o'clock at night,
at the office. The same feeling had im-
pelled me on other occasions to take part
in the administrative work of public
bodies; but though I discharged these

duties punctiliously, I never either then or later found in that sort of work the satisfaction which comes from giving one's whole mind to a task in the conviction that one can do it well and that one is putting into it the best of oneself. For this reason I have never sought such work and have indeed always refused it except when I have failed to find any one else to undertake it, as willing as myself and more suited to it by nature; and this has been, and is, my constant rule. Six months later, relieved of this labour, I began, and in September finished, my *Theory and History of Aesthetic*,[1] which was sent to press in November, and published in April 1902.

Two things were borne in upon me as I read the proofs of this book : first, that I could not leave the matter there, without adding detailed developments, appli-

---

[1] *Èstetica come scienza dell' espressione e linguistica generale*: Laterza, 1902; 4th ed., 1912. E. T. *Aesthetic, &c.*, 1909; 2nd ed., 1922.

cations, and illustrations, and plunging into discussion and controversy; secondly, that this book, into which I imagined that I had emptied all the philosophy which had accumulated in my head, had in fact filled my head with fresh philosophy, with doubts and problems concerning especially the other forms of the spirit, the theories of which I had outlined in their relation to aesthetic, and the general conception of reality. I thought accordingly of treating this book as a sort of programme or outline to be completed on the one hand by the publication of a review, and, on the other, by means of a series of books, theoretical and historical, which should serve to define my philosophical position more precisely. My friend Gentile and I had often discussed the desirability of a new review, with a definite intellectual policy; but I had delayed taking any steps until the completion of my Aesthetic should set me free to turn my energies elsewhere. In the summer of 1902 it seemed to me that the time had come; and I planned *La Critica*, an historical, literary, and philosophical review, and drew up a prospectus in which I defined the principles which I undertook to propagate and defend, and those which I proposed to attack. To prevent its becoming a monotonous string of dry reviews or a disjointed collection of essays on all kinds of subjects, I resolved to print articles dealing with the intellectual life of Italy during the last fifty years, the period when the modern Italian State and modern Italy were coming into existence. I thought, moreover, that the interest which this subject must excite would make it an excellent text for my sermon, in other words, for theoretical discussions. I entrusted the history of Italian philosophy during that period to Gentile, and made myself responsible for the corresponding history of literature. It was a step that cost me much misgiving, for I had hitherto regarded this modern

literature only from the point of view
of an ordinary reader, taking an interest
in it but thinking little about it ; and I
feared that my disposition, and my absorption at the moment in philosophical
questions, qualified me very ill for the
office of literary critic in the proper sense.
But the subject called aloud for treatment, and I could find no one among my
friends fitted to treat it ; so I began to
deal with it myself, not without timidity
and hesitation, as the earliest articles
prove, but taking comfort from the
reflection that at least I had cleared
the ground of prejudices, stated certain
problems clearly, and opened the way to
better critics and historians than myself.
Indeed, though I afterwards acquired a
certain confidence, partly through finding
that people agreed with my views, partly
through the work itself, an exercise
favourable to the formation of definite
opinions, and especially through seeing
that others, my rivals and merciless critics,

did no better than myself and only used more words and a more high-flown style, I still feel that these early essays have a peculiar interest, rather as illustrations of an aesthetical theory than as a book primarily intended for an analysis of the inner spirit of modern literature. Had that been my aim, I should have treated them in another way, as indeed I did treat those of them, or those parts of them, in which this strictly historical motive came to predominate.

The foundation of *La Critica,* the prospectus of which was published in November 1902 and its first number in the January following, marked the beginning of a new period in my life, the period of maturity or harmony between myself and reality. For years I had suffered almost continuously from a conflict between what I was doing and what I felt, though confusedly, that I ought to be doing; a division between my practical and my theoretical self, the latter reading and

writing, the former idling or seeking satisfaction in various scattered and disconnected ways; between a kind of studies
devoid of any real utility and the voice
of conscience upbraiding me and urging
me on towards another goal. But as I
worked at *La Critica*, there grew up within
me the calm conviction that I was in my
right place and was giving the best that
I had; that I was engaged in politics, in
the broad sense of that word, doing the
work at once of a student and of a citizen;
so that I need no longer blush, as I had
often blushed in the past, on meeting a
politician or a socially active fellow-
townsman. Not that I prided myself on
my performance; when, some years later
and for some years together, I heard myself called the master and spiritual guide
of the younger generation, it was with surprise and at times with annoyance; but
I was glad to be at last using my powers,
whether great or small, to the full. The
ideal at which I aimed was derived not

from my personality but from my varied
experience ; having lived enough in the
academic world to recognize both its
virtues and its failings, and having at
the same time kept fresh my feelings for
real life and for literature and science
as arising out of it and renewing themselves in it, I directed my criticisms and
attacks in part against the amateurs and
anti-methodical workers, and in part
against academics with all their comfort-
able prejudices and their easy-going con-
templation of art and science from the
outside.

To edit and in part to write *La Critica*
was the most direct service that I could
render to Italian culture ; but in the years
that followed I was able to contribute
further towards the same end by publishing collections or series of volumes. At
first I undertook this task unaided, and
issued two volumes of a collection of
' studies ' ; later I was able to work on a
much larger scale and with much more

success, owing to the energy of a young Apulian publisher, Laterza of Bari, who had applied to me for advice. Thus arose in 1906 the collection of 'Classics of Modern Philosophy', conceived by Gentile and edited by himself and by me, and later that of 'Writers of Italy' and others of less importance; and several books were by my doing or at my suggestion printed or reprinted in the 'Library of Modern Culture', which Laterza had already set on foot before I came to know him. A large proportion of these consisted of works by Southern writers of the Risorgimento and the early years of the Unity, who till then were almost unknown.

For all this, I did not lose sight of my more strictly scientific task, the development and completion of the body of ideas contained implicitly in my *Aesthetic* and now pressing upon my mind with the numerous problems which that work had brought to light. Thus, by following my usual custom of preparing all the material for *La Critica* a year or two, or even three years, in advance, I found time to attend to what I regard as my chief works, and was able to publish my first draft of Logic [1] in 1905, my essay on Hegel [2] in 1906, a sketch of my 'Philosophy of Law as Economics' [3] in 1907, the complete 'Philosophy of Practice' [4] in 1908, and the 'Logic' [5] in its fully-developed form in 1909. After these came in 1910 the 'Problems of Aesthetic', [6] in 1911 the monograph on Vico, [7] the philosopher

[1] *Logica come scienza del concetto puro*: Laterza, 1905.

[2] *Ciò che è vivo e ciò che è morto della filosofia di Hegel*: Laterza, 1906: out of print: reprinted in *Saggio sull' Hegel*, &c., Laterza, 1913. E. T. *What is living, &c.*, Macmillan, 1915.

[3] Incorporated in the *Filosofia della Pratica*.

[4] *Filosofia della Pratica*: Laterza, 1908; ed. 3, 1922. E. T. *Philosophy of the Practical*, Macmillan, 1913.

[5] *Logica come scienza del concetto puro*: Laterza, 1909. E. T. *Logic, &c.*, Macmillan, 1917.

[6] *Problemi di estetica e contributi alla storia dell'estetica italiana*: Laterza, 1910; ed. 2, 1924.

[7] *La filosofia di Giambattista Vico*: Laterza, 1911;

most closely akin to myself, a volume preceded and accompanied by philological, bibliographical, and editorial work on the same philosopher, in 1912 the first essays on the 'Theory of History',[1] in 1913 the others on the same subject and the 'Handbook of Aesthetic'.[2] And I have lately completed, as the natural sequel to my essays on the theory of history, a detailed history of 'Historical Thought in Italy, from the beginning of the eighteenth century to the present day',[3] to be published by instalments in the second series of *La Critica*, beginning this year [1915]. To these must be added numerous monographs and single essays, and many editions by me of texts

E. T. *Philosophy of Vico*, Howard Latimer, 1913; reissue, *Giambattista Vico*, Allen and Unwin.

[1] *Teoria e storia della storiografia*: Laterza, 1913; ed. 2, 1920. E. T. *Theory and history of historiography*, 1921.

[2] *Breviario di Estetica*: Laterza, 1912. E. T. *The Essence of Aesthetic*, 1921.

[3] *Storia della storiografia italiana dagli inizi del secolo decimonono ai giorni nostri*: Laterza, 1921.

and documents which were, or still are, of use to me in the pursuit of my chief object.

I have given the barest outline of the work done in the last twelve years, the most fruitful of my whole life hitherto, for the simple reason that it represents my escape from the difficulties of the earlier years, the solution of my internal conflicts, my achieving of peace; a peace which, so far as it is peace, has in it little to relate. And by peace I do not mean idleness or pleasure-seeking, but harmonious, coherent, self-confident labour and exertion; nor do I mean to separate the two processes of education and production, as if I had at first learnt and were now simply putting what I had learnt into practice. What I had really, as I think, learnt at the beginning of this period was the art of learning without dissipating my energies, as I formerly did, in a barren external addition of fact to fact; the art of learning as my inmost needs moved me, guided by principles, conscious of difficulties, ready to wait in patience and allow my thoughts to ripen. Hence I have found by experience and in my own person the falsity of that pedagogic theory which restricts education to the first part of life, the preface of the book, and the truth of the opposite doctrine which conceives the inner life as a perpetual education, and knowledge as the unity of knowing and learning. To know and to have lost the power of learning, to be educated and to be unable still to improve one's education, is to bring one's life to a standstill, and the right name for that is not life but death.

III. INTELLECTUAL DEVELOPMENT.

AS I have said, I first read the works of De Sanctis as a schoolboy in the *liceo*; and even then they made a deep impression upon me and led me to practise literary criticism in my school essays. But if I had fully understood the thought of De Sanctis, grasping it in its fundamental conception and in each separate judgement, and apprehending the varied and coherent experience which had dictated it and could alone render it intelligible, I should have been *lusus naturae*, an old head on young shoulders, or rather just De Sanctis himself transformed from an old man into a lad. The fact is, that all I could pick up from De Sanctis was a point here and there; and in especial, though in a very crude shape, this central idea : that art is not a work of reflection and logic, nor yet a product of skill, but pure and spontaneous imaginative form. The philosophical basis of this idea, its necessary implications, the general conception to which it belongs, and its bearings on judgement and action, all these I saw darkly, if at all, and only began by degrees to discern as time went on. Even yet, perhaps, I have not fully developed and recognized them.

There is a certain falsely abstract way of imagining the relation between a thought and its predecessor; an error closely connected with the false view of educational progress. It consists in thinking of this relation as if a mind in its early years acquired a precise knowledge of all that had been hitherto accomplished, and then proceeded to criticize, correct, and supplement, on the strength of this firmly-established position. But actual development takes place in a quite different manner. It begins, one might almost say, not by understanding but by misunderstanding, or not only by under-

standing but also by failing to understand.
The spirit achieves its progress by solving
new problems, different from those which
once occupied men's thoughts; and among
the new problems is the work of these
earlier men themselves, which at first
stands over against the spirit of to-day
as a 'thing-in-itself', that is, nothing, and
then by degrees enters into it and forms
part of it, as a problem to be solved.
Hence to understand one's predecessors
and to progress beyond them are not two
distinct phases but one and the same phase,
not two processes but a single process.

The general problem at which I can
now see myself to have been working for
many years may be stated as the problem
of the appropriating and assimilating De
Sanctis' thought by a mind very differently
disposed from his own; a mind eager to
make precise what in him remained vague,
to bind into systematic coherence all the
questions treated by philosophy in the
course of its history, including those that

have arisen since De Sanctis' own day,
and thus to create a philosophy where
he had only left critical essays and sketches
of literary history, and, as a result of this
deepening and consolidation of philosophical thought, to create a new critcism
and a new history—new in many of their
details, and new in their general character.
The means to this end, or the leaven of
this ferment, could only be the complete
working-out, in itself and in all its relations, of this conception of art, which
came to me first in abstract isolation and
was now by degrees to shape for itself a
body less inadequate than that which it
possessed for De Sanctis, and differently
organized. But I need hardly say that,
problem and solution being notoriously
one, this general problem did not exist
for me in a conscious and actual manner,
in my own attitude towards the life of
thought ; and that this problem is simply
the life of thought itself, as I lived it
actually and in detail, down to the point

at which it succeeded in formulating itself
to itself at once as a general problem and
as a general solution.

To these difficulties and complications,
which beset the course of every real
development, is due the fact that an ardent
reader of De Sanctis like myself, who
ought to have known by heart every word
of his doctrine that erudition without
philosophy is neither criticism nor history
but mere formless matter (and no doubt
I did know every word of it, but not by
heart, for I repeated the words without
grasping their full sense), could spend so
long in the pursuit of erudition without
philosophy, in mere antiquarianism. I
actually enjoyed it, partly because of my
inborn taste for study and love of books,
partly because it was the fashion of the
day, and I not only followed the fashion
but, with that logical consistency which
was part of my intellectual character,
exaggerated it. Yet, if I had not done
this, I could never have thoroughly and

firmly understood De Sanctis' central
thought, the transcending of mere erudition ; for such an understanding is in-
separable from the experience of that
which is to be transcended, which must
first have been lived in one's own person :
and further, I could never have worked
out in detail the relation and the distinction between historical criticism and aesthetic criticism, and between erudition
and history in general, as I have done
where I distinguish, for instance, scholarship from philological history and philological history from poetic history, and
all these from history in the strict and
proper sense of the word, historical history. Again and again, as I laid bare the
weaknesses of 'eruditism' or 'philo-
logism', its inner contradictions, its laugh-
able illusions, I have said to myself, 'Many
readers will fancy that in framing this
psychological type, in drawing this cari-
cature, I have derived my material from
one or another of the philologists I criti-

cize; but my real material I have found within myself; the real type is my own person, remembering as I do what I once believed, or at least what once flitted through my mind, only to be driven away by common sense, when I was working as a mere scholar and antiquary'.

To the same cause is due the fact that, though I might have found in De Sanctis, as now I do, a sane and simple morality, austere without exaggeration and lofty without fanaticism, I first wavered for years in the most agonizing perplexity and then settled down for a time in a conception inferior to that of De Sanctis, a Herbartian scholasticism in which the moral ideal was energetically affirmed, but affirmed as a thing not of this world, a thing exalted above man as above a dead matter to be stamped with its own mark as approved or disapproved, or stamped now more clearly, now less. Yet however I have subsequently criti- cized and ridiculed this conception—and,

here again, ridiculed myself, my own past
—the fact remains that this abstract rigorism was a road which I must needs travel
if I was to understand concrete morality
and raise it to the level of a philosophical
theory. And this rigorism, which was at
the same time a passion for sharp distinctions, not only saved me from associa-
tionism and positivism and evolutionism,
but equally put me on my guard against
falling into the errors of a half-naturalistic
and half mystical Hegelianism, which
with its restless and often mythological
dialectic annulled or weakened the very
distinctions whose life gave life to the
dialectical process.

This Platonic or scholastic or Herbartian conception not only protected me
against the prevailing naturalism and
materialism of my youth and armed me
for the future, but it also rendered me
absolutely proof against the wiles of sen-
sationalism and decadentism, which were
at that time beginning to assert themselves

and were soon to find a representative
figure in a man of my own district and
almost of my own age, but not of my own
religion : Gabriele D'Annunzio. I cannot remember that I ever for a single
moment lost my hold on the distinction
between sensuous refinement and spiritual
fineness, erotic flights and moral elevation,
sham heroism and stern duty; and though
here and there D'Annunzio's art won my
admiration, I never felt even a fleeting
and sentimental agreement with the ethics
which he suggested or preached outright.
The kinship or resemblance between
D'Annunzio's work and my own, of which
young critics have more than once written,
is a mere product of their fancy, and gives
ground for suspecting that these critics
fail to make the distinction mentioned
above, which to me has always been
perfectly sharp. D'Annunzio and I are
spiritually of two different races; and
in any case it would have been difficult
for him to influence my mind, because

people commonly influence not their contemporaries, but their juniors. In fact, D'Annunzianism in the proper sense is a thing of the generation that has grown up since 1890. My generation was, if anything, Carduccian.

Another fancy or mistaken guess that I must mention is my 'Hegelianism', a supposed family tradition handed on to me by the notorious Hegelian Bertrando Spaventa, my cousin on the father's side. I have already described the complete estrangement between Spaventa and my family; but even when, during my stay in his brother Silvio's house at Rome, I took up Bertrando Spaventa's books for the first time and tried to read them, they rather turned me against Hegelianism than introduced me to it. Besides, I was just then attending with great enthusiasm the University lectures of the Herbartian and anti-Hegelian Labriola, and greedily drinking his words in conversation at Spaventa's house or in the street as I walked with him from the University ; and Labriola's mocking and malicious tongue spared neither his former teacher of philosophy nor the philosophy that his teacher had defended. But though Labriola's authority carried much weight with me at that age, the fundamental reason for my failure to enjoy Spaventa's works was the profound difference of temperament between myself and him. Spaventa came to philosophy from the church and from theology ; for him, the chief and almost the only problem was always that of the relation between being and knowing, the problem of transcendence and immanence, the specifically theologico-philosophical problem ; whereas I, when once I had overcome the sentimental regrets caused by my abandonment of religion, soon settled down into a kind of unconscious immanentism, caring for no other world than that in which I actually lived, and not conscious, in any direct or primary way, of the problem of transcendence. Hence I found no difficulty in conceiving the relation between thought and being; my difficulty, if I had felt a difficulty, would have been the opposite one, how to conceive a being apart from thought or a thought apart from being. The problems that really interested me, and compelled me to philosophize through my yearning for light, were those of art, of the moral life, of law, and, later, of historical method—the task at which I proposed to work. This living need found no satisfaction in Spaventa's writings; and they repelled me, in addition, by their arid and abstract style, at once dry and laboured, and in complete contrast with the style of De Sanctis, simple, popular, packed with realities, never losing its contact with actual life. Nor did it occur to me, at that time, to look for Hegel in Hegel himself, partly because my insufficient philosophical training would

hardly have allowed it, partly because
Spaventa's pages had thoroughly fright-
ened me : for (I argued in those days) if
the interpreter and commentator is so
difficult, what must the original text
be ? Years of experience were needed to
convince me that interpreters and commentators are as a rule far more obscure
than the authors they interpret. I must
add that the Hegelian philosophy of
history outraged my scholar's sense of
decency; and thus, although in absorb-
ing De Sanctis' theory of art I had assimi-
lated a great deal of sound Vician and
Hegelian idealism, I was quite unconscious of the fact, and actually tried
to fit this theory of art into a frame
of Herbartian philosophy. In this attempt I was encouraged by Labriola, who
once admitted to me that in aesthetic
the Herbartians had not gained such
good results as the idealists, and later
advised me to read some eclectic Herbartians who had tried to modify their

Herbartian principles by a compromise with the aesthetic of the Idea.

My state of mind, as an idealist of De Sanctis' school in aesthetic, a Herbartian in ethics and the general conception of values, an anti-Hegelian and anti-metaphysician in the theory of history and the general conception of the world, a naturalist or intellectualist in the theory of knowledge—these elements being neither harmonized nor yet confused with one another, but merely set side by side in a provisional order, with gaps between them—may be seen reflected in a few short articles published twenty years ago and collected in the volume of *Iuvenilia* mentioned above, and, in a later form, as modified by the internal conflict that grew out of my antiquarian studies, in my first philosophical essays on *The Concept of History* and *Literary Criticism*; and traces of it still appear from time to time in some of my works of the period immediately

following. The ferment of Hegelianism
made its way into my thought late in
life, at first through Marxianism and
historical materialism, which had bridged
the gulf that separated my master Labriola from Hegel and dialectic, and
similarly taught me what a wealth of
concrete history, however arbitrarily and
artificially treated, was contained in the
Hegelian philosophy. But I regarded
even the Hegel to whom the interpreta-
tions and adaptations of Marx and Engels
introduced me, with a suspicious and
critical eye; as appears from my essays
on historical materialism, in which I
set myself to purge that doctrine of
every trace of abstract *a priori* thought,
whether in the form of 'philosophy of
history' or in that of the later 'evolutionism', and to defend the value of the
Kantian ethics and reject the mystery of
a substructure or Economy—the Idea in
disguise—operating beneath the level
of consciousness, and a superstructure or

consciousness described as a superficial phenomenon. I came into more direct touch with Hegel through the friendship and collaboration of Gentile, in whom the tradition of Spaventa came to life again more flexible, more modern, more open to criticism and self-criticism, richer in spiritual interests; and in this way, in spite of occasional differences between the paths which we respectively followed, Gentile and myself came to influence each other and to correct each other's faults.

But it was only the violent effort of thought entailed, as I have said, by my *Aesthetic* that enabled me to vanquish, of myself and for myself, the naturalism and Herbartianism that still fettered me: to vanquish the logic of naturalism by appeal to the logic of grades of the spirit, or of development, which alone enabled me to grasp the relation between words and thought, imagination and intellect, utility and morality; to

vanquish a naturalistic transcendence
by the criticisms which I was irresistibly
accumulating against the literary kinds,
grammar, the separate arts, and the rhetorical styles; for these criticisms enabled me to lay my finger on the point
at which 'nature', the product of man's
own spirit, is introduced into the pure
spiritual world of art, and led me by
degrees, having thus denied the reality
of nature in art, to deny it everywhere
and to discover everywhere its true character, not as reality but as the product
of abstracting thought. In short, I freed
myself from what in after years I came
to call the dualism of values, as opposed
to the dualism of spirit and nature, by
the conclusion to which I was led in
studying the aesthetic and all other forms
of judgement : namely that true thought
is simply thought, beautiful expression
simply expression, and so forth, and that
false thought and ugly expression are
non-thought and non-expression, the not-

being which has no reality apart from the dialectical moment which posits and dissolves it.

The essay on *Fundamental Propositions* and the first edition of the *Aesthetic* retain traces of a certain naturalism, or rather Kantianism, which here and there conjures up once more the ghost of nature, and states distinctions, at any rate so far as choice of words and imagery is concerned, somewhat abstractly. But when I had published the *Aesthetic* and sketched a logic, I felt that the time had come for a closer acquaintance with this Hegel, whose doctrines I had hitherto rather sampled than studied in their entirety. And now I met with another proof of the truth, that books which remain dumb and unintelligible to a reader who has never worked for himself at a subject connected with their own, become charged with power when they begin to converse with us and help us to clarify half-formed thoughts of our own, to

change into conceptions our own pre-
sentiments of conceptions, to support
and encourage us in the way that we have
already taken or at which we have all
but arrived. When—it was in 1905—I
plunged into the reading of Hegel, throw-
ing aside his pupils and commentators, I
seemed to be plunging into myself, to be
at grips with my own consciousness. Yet
even now I was no 'Hegelian', precisely
because I had come to the study of Hegel
with a varied cultural experience behind
me, and with a ready-formed philosophical system which already included in
itself a criticism of certain Hegelian doctrines and their replacement by sounder
views. At the point which I had now
reached, indeed, I could no longer adopt
the essentially youthful attitude of taking
on trust a half-understood doctrine, without criticizing and reconstructing it from
within, merely because it is heard on
the lips of one's chosen guide, or of a
teacher who, by opening his pupil's mind

to one truth, disposes him to believe blindly or almost blindly in whatever he says, even if it has not as yet, for the pupil, the self-evidence of truth. It is an attitude which I have often observed in men of great worth; it was Spaventa's attitude towards a great part of the Hegelian system, which he tried to accept without ever really accepting, and yet repeated it and retained it provisionally; but it was never mine, except just in those years of my youth when, as a pupil of Labriola, I adopted as a matter of faith, and respected without truly making it my own, the theory of the 'five' practical ideas 'each indeducible from the rest', and so forth. But in 1905, to study Hegel and turn him to my own use meant criticizing and dissolving him; and therefore the outcome of my study was the essay *What is living and what is dead in Hegel's Philosophy*, thought out towards the end of 1905, written in the spring and published in the summer of 1906.

About the same time I also read the
modern theories of scientific knowledge
and the confused utterances of the prag-
matists, in which I found fresh confirma-
tion of criticisms I had already made while
working at aesthetic doctrines, and whose
criticisms I saw to be in places akin to those
levelled by Hegel against the 'abstract
intellect'; but I emphatically rejected
the intuitionist or pragmatist solution
of philosophical problems, just as I had
rejected the abstractly speculative solution offered by Hegel.

The conception to which my criticism
of Hegel and my general review of the
history of philosophy led me, was summed
up in the general title of *Philosophy as the
Science of Spirit*, which I gave to my three
volumes or treatises on Aesthetic, Logic,
and Practice. This conception has often
been called 'Hegelianism', or 'neo-Hegel-
ianism', especially by people who only
know Hegel by hearsay and therefore,
naturally, detest him; but it might as

well, and with equal justice, be called a
new positivism, a new Kantianism, a new
value-philosophy, a new Vicianism, and
so forth ; and all these titles, like the first,
would fail to hit its peculiar character,
which is clearly enough indicated by the
history of its origin as I have here set it
down. If the most important things in
Hegel's philosophy are considered to be
the conception of a Logos that realizes
itself unconsciously in the world of Nature and rediscovers itself in the world
of Spirit ; and the allied conception of
a Logic of this Logos, traversing a long
chain of dialectical triads in order to
culminate in the Idea and thence to
plunge into Nature ; and that of a
Phenomenology preceding this Logic and
forming as it were the ladder by which
the logical empyrean is reached ; and,
lastly, the *a priori* construction of nature
and human history and similar pseudo-
metaphysical undertakings to which
Hegel's pupils and imitators have chiefly

devoted themselves—and these are the things which in the past have generally been thought the most important—then philosophy as the science of spirit, as outlined by me, is not the continuation but the utter overthrow of Hegelianism. For it denies the distinction between Phenomenology and Logic; it denies the dialectical construction not only of the philosophies of nature and history but of Logic as well; and it denies the triad of Logos, Nature, and Spirit and asserts the sole reality of Spirit, in which nature is nothing but an aspect in the dialectic of spirit itself. But if, on the contrary, the important things in Hegel are considered to be his powerful tendency towards immanence and concreteness, and his conception of a philosophical logic fundamentally different from the logic of naturalism, then philosophy as the science of spirit certainly recognizes in Hegel not so much its father (for clearly it can have no father except its own author) as its great forerunner; and in Vico another, more remote and not less venerable. Titles like these, however, are of little importance, and their chief utility is to those who wish to save themselves the trouble of studying a thought of which they are ignorant by including it in another with which they are acquainted or, more often, conveniently fancy themselves acquainted.

As I dealt in succession with the various parts of the philosophy of spirit, these features gradually grew clearer; contradictions revealed themselves and had to be resolved; and the parts came to agree better with each other and the whole. Hence arose that progress of my thought which went unceasingly forward from the *Aesthetic* to the *Logic*, thence to the *Philosophy of Practice* and the second edition or rather reconstruction of the *Logic*, the *Handbook of Aesthetic*, the essays on the *Theory and History of Historical Thought*, and the works which are follow-

ing them and will follow them in the
future. To mention the chief points only,
this progress appeared in the gradual
elimination of naturalism, the growing
emphasis laid upon spiritual unity, and
the deepening of the meaning attached
to the conception of intuition in aesthetic,
now elaborated into that of lyrism.
Above all, in the course of this labour I
have learnt by personal experience the
impossibility of holding to the old idea
of truth as a thing attained once for all,
even as the reward of age-long efforts and
by the genius of a single discoverer : an
idea which persisted in my *Aesthetic* not
as a positive affirmation, for here and
there it wavered and threatened to col-
lapse, but as an unconscious and partial
prejudice not yet overcome, and appearing especially in the somewhat crude
treatment of the history of that subject.
To-day, I observe in my own case the
impossibility of resting upon the results of
past thought; I see a new crop of problems

springing up in a field from which I have but now reaped a harvest of solutions; I find myself calling in question the conclusions to which I have previously come; and these facts, which appear in every part of philosophy as I handle and re-handle it, force me to recognize that truth will not let itself be tied fast for ever. They teach me modesty towards my present thoughts, which tomorrow will appear deficient and in need of correction, and indulgence towards my self of yesterday or the past, whose thoughts, however inadequate in the eyes of my present self, yet contained some real element of truth: and this modesty and indulgence pass into a sense of piety towards thinkers of the past, whom now I am careful not to blame, as once I blamed them, for their inability to do what no man, however great, can do —to close the eternal gates of truth, to fix into eternity the fleeting moment. Another lesson that I learned by experience was that every progress in my thought was effected not by insisting upon the terms of the problems I had solved, but by the growth of new problems; and that these, though built upon the foundation of the old, were not their immediate consequence, but were excited by new impulses of feeling and new conditions of life. Thus, for instance, the conversion of my first concept of intuition into the further concept of pure or lyrical intuition was not due to an inference from the first, which taken by itself satisfied me and remained inert, but to suggestions arising from the actual practice of literary criticism, as I wrote my notes on modern Italian literature and reflected directly upon works of art and tried to harmonize my former thoughts with the new thoughts that thus arose. Lastly, as I worked at my *Philosophy of Practice* and inquired into the relation between intention and action, my denial of any such dualism and of the conceivability of an intention without action led me to think once more of the dualism which I had left standing in the first *Logic* between the concept and the singular judgement, that is, between philosophy as antecedent and history as consequent; and I realized that a concept which was not at the same time a judgement of the particular was as unreal as an intention that was not at the same time an action. Then I remembered the long discussions between Gentile and myself, a few years before, concerning the Hegelian formula which identifies philosophy with the history of philosophy. I had rejected it, and Gentile had defended it, but his defence had not convinced me; now I was disposed to agree with Gentile, but on condition that I might interpret the formula freely in my own way, in other words, conformably to my notion of Spirit, in which philosophy is one moment, and thus convert it into the formula identifying philosophy with history, which I worked out in the second edition of the *Logic*.

This conclusion has exerted great influence not only on the later development of my thought, but upon my whole spiritual life; for it has had the effect of finally setting me free from scepticism toward myself and toward man's power of reaching the truth. For however conceited a philosopher is (and I have never been conceited, in spite of certain movements of impatience and a certain briskness in controversy which others may have mistaken for conceit), how can he ever claim that he has 'discovered' the truth all by himself, in the system he propounds, a truth unknown to all previous ages? And however dull and slow-witted he may be—even if he is as slow-witted as Schopenhauer himself!—how can he fail to notice that his lack of movement is only apparent or approximate, and that he himself is in a constant process of developing and partially negating what he once affirmed? That being so, scepticism is inevitable and invincible, given the concept of a static reality outside the historical process. But the concept of truth as history tempers the conceit of to-day and opens up hopes for to-morrow; for the despairing sense of struggling in vain to pursue a quarry that always flies and hides, it substitutes the consciousness of always possessing a wealth that always increases; for the melancholy picture of a blind humanity groping in the darkness it substitutes the heroic picture of mankind rising from light to light.

Firm in this conviction, I care nothing for the fate of my ' philosophy ', which others call a system and I a series of attempts at a system; I open all the doors of my mind to doubts and to the voice of every new experience, sure that the fruit of it, while correcting the thoughts that I falsely imagine myself to have had, can never destroy what I have once really thought, and that this, therefore, is true for ever and will even find its truth confirmed and enriched by new truths which at first I could not think because their conditions were not yet formed within me and the need for them had not yet arisen. Many of my friends, when I had published the whole of the *Philosophy of Spirit*, advised me to rest now that I had, as they said, completed my 'system'; but I knew that I had completed nothing, closed nothing, but only written a few volumes about the problems which ever since my youth had been by degrees accumulating in my spirit. And I went on living my life, and reading not so much the philosophers as the poets and historians; and soon I found growing up within me, of themselves, my reflections on *the Philosophy of Vico*, my essays on the *Theory and History of Historical Thought*, the *Ethical Fragments*,[1] and the studies in the *History of Historical Thought in Italy*; all thoughts which break the fancied bounds of the system and yield, under close scrutiny, new systems or new

[1] *Frammenti di Etica*, Laterza, 1921.

attempts at a system, since whenever we take a step everything moves. I shall do the same thing again; I shall go on philosophizing, even if, as I sometimes allow myself to think, not without pleasure, I one day give up 'philosophy', philosophy ordinarily so called in the narrow or scholastic sense of the word, treatises, dissertations, debates, historical inquiries into the doctrines of so-called philosophers; for the unity of philosophy and history means just this, that all thought is philosophy, whatever it is about and in whatever form it is cast. Indeed, the highest form of philosophy consists, as I believe, in overcoming the provisional form of abstract 'theory' and thinking the philosophy of particular facts, narrating history; a history that is not merely *narrated* but *thought*.

IV. A GLANCE AROUND ME AND
BEFORE ME

IF at this point I were asked what effect my work had produced, I could fill many pages with details concerning the circulation of my books both in and out of Italy; the discussions, sometimes amounting to bitter controversy, which they have excited; and the numerous works to which they have given rise in the various regions traversed by my thought—aesthetic, the philosophy of language, the history of literature, the history of art, logic, the theory of history, ethics, economics and politics, the theory of law, and so forth. Accustomed to make extracts and notes of everything connected with the authors for whom I have an especial affection—a fact that explains the bibliographies I have published—I do the same for myself; for I study myself, and have a certain not unnatural affection for myself; and hence I should have no lack of material which, properly displayed, would give me the pleasure of a father and grandfather who sees gathered round him a fine family of children and grandchildren. But if I were to do this, I should be writing those memoirs which I had determined not to write because I could not see their value or, indeed, their necessity; and I should, further, dislike writing them since, though I do not fall into the extravagance of hating myself, I am not disposed to talk about myself when I cannot see what purpose I should thereby serve. And I did think that this attempt to analyse my ethical and intellectual development would serve a purpose; which is the reason why I made it.

The question may, however, bear another and more intimate meaning: namely, what effect my theories have produced on modern thought. But to that I must reply by recalling a prin-

ciple whose value I have tested in my
studies of the history of philosophy :.
that to imagine a thought as producing
effects is to conceive thought, and
indeed all life, naturalistically and
mechanically. What a thought really
produces is never an effect, but always a
collaboration; and just as the thought
of a single writer is born of the collaboration of earlier with contemporary
history, so that same thought, when
(as we inaccurately say) it issues from
him and communicates itself to others,
passes through an historical development
that is no longer his, but that of all who
welcome it and improve upon it, or even
reject it and misunderstand it and con-
trovert it and ignore it : in a word, think
for themselves. Descartes did not pro-
duce rationalism and the French Revolution; it was the spirit of the world
that actualized itself successively in Car-
tesianism, Encyclopaedism, and the
Revolution. To answer the question in

this latter sense, therefore, I should have to write an essay on the history of thought in my lifetime, as I should have had to write an essay on the history of culture to answer it in the former sense. This was not what I set out to do; and I do not think that this is the right place for it.

Lastly, the question may have a third meaning, which I will call psychological : am I satisfied or dissatisfied, content or discontented, with my work and the welcome that the world has given it ? With my work, as is again only natural, I am both satisfied and dissatisfied ; with its reception I am well content, because I am in the habit of recognizing whatever happens as rational ; and in a more contingent and popular sense I am more than content, for I never imagined that I should gain the ear of so large a public as that which I now see around me. I never remember to have cherished ambitous dreams in my youth ; on the contrary, I remember that my ideals were extremely simple. When I had written the *Aesthetic*, I insisted upon limiting the edition to five hundred copies, and in establishing *La Critica* I reckoned upon a couple of hundred kindly readers. So everything has surpassed, I will not say my hopes, but my expectations. And I have never strongly felt any hopes or desires except—perhaps I may be allowed to say it, for it is true—the desire to find my way out of darkness into light.

And even now, the darkness gathers closer and closer round my mind. But the acute anguish from which I suffered so much in my youth is to-day a chronic anguish; once wild and ungovernable, it has become domesticated and tame; for, as I said, I now know its symptoms, its remedy, and its natural course, and therefore I have won the calm which the ripeness of years brings to men who have achieved that ripeness by labour.

This calm has further enabled me for

the past fifteen years to sketch in advance from time to time, with tolerable exactness, the programme which I was to pursue, roughly for the next four or five years and more accurately for the next two or three. The unexpected has played little part in my work during these fifteen years, and I have allowed myself to be influenced by circumstances seldom, and only in little things. This year I am less certain of my course. It is a year which I had set aside for revising, arranging, and correcting all my youthful works, preparing materials for certain editorial labours, and setting my private affairs in order. Much of this I have done already, and I expect to finish it all before the end of the year. It was to be a kind of 'liquidation of the past', designed to procure me the necessary peace of mind to pursue and intensify the work which I had already begun upon historical thought, for which I hoped, by means of theories, instances, and controversies, to do something like what I had done, or nearly done, for philosophical thought, aesthetic, and literary criticism. In especial, I had in mind a work on the historical development of the nineteenth century so far as that development still lives in the present state of our civilization; a history that should join hands with action. But as I write these lines, the war rages around me, and may well involve Italy; and I cannot see what tasks will be forced upon me or what duties assigned to me, even in the near future, by this gigantic war, whose course and remoter effects are still obscure, this war which may issue in world-wide disturbance or in sheer exhaustion. My mind hangs in suspense; its image mirrored in the future wavers distortedly, like a reflection upon stormy water.